Myths and Legends of The Age Of CHIVALRY

Abigail Frost
Illustrated by Francis Phillipps

MARSHALL CAVENDISH
New York · London · Toronto · Sydney

Library Edition Published 1990

Published by Marshall Cavendish Corporation
147 West Merrick Road
Freeport, Long Island
N.Y. 11520

Library edition produced by DPM
Printed by Colorcraft Ltd. in Hong Kong.

©Marshall Cavendish Corporation 1990
©Cherrytree Press Ltd. 1989

Adapted by AS Publishing from La Chevalerie, published by Hachette.

Library of Congress Cataloging-in-Publication Data

Frost, Abigail.

 The Age of Chivalry / by Abigail Frost.
  p. cm. - (Myths and legends)
 Includes index
 Summary: Presents legends of King Arthur and Charlemagne
 ISBN 1-85435-235-0 (lib. bdg.)
  1. Arthurian romances. 2. Charlemagne, Emporer,742-814-Romances. [1. Arthur, King. 2. Charlemagne, Emporer, 742-814. 3. Knights and knighthood - Folklore. 4. Folklore - England. 5. Folklore - Europe.] I. Malory, Thomas, Sir, 15th cent. Mort d'Arthur. II. Title. III.Series: Frost, Abigail, Myths and legends.
PZ8.1.F926Ag 1990
398.22'094 - dc20   89-17396
                                                             CIP
                                                             AC

CONTENTS

ARThUR

Among the most enduring legends of Britain are those of King Arthur and his Knights of the Round Table.

Arthur himself would never have come into the world if it had not been for a magician called Merlin. Merlin was born when the Devil decided to play a trick on humans. He took the form of a man and courted a beautiful, but foolish, young girl. The poor frightened girl discovered that she was expecting a baby. Her parents asked her who the father was, but she did not even know his name. The laws of the time were harsh; she was condemned to death.

However, the judges agreed to save the unborn baby, who was innocent of any sin, so the girl was imprisoned until the baby was born. It was a boy, who was named Merlin. The baby Merlin was covered with hair, which frightened away all the women who were asked to nurse him. So he was left with his mother in prison, until her day of execution. Then Merlin, only a few weeks old, showed his strange power for the first time.

As the jailers came to take away his mother, the baby Merlin spoke, saying that his mother had committed no crime, and ordered them to set her free.

Merlin grew up with strange powers. He could read people's minds, see the past and predict the future.

ARTHUR'S BRITAIN

Britain was ruled by Vortigern, a wicked usurper who had seized power and invited Saxon invaders to the land. The true heir, Uther Pendragon, had escaped to France.

Vortigern, who lived in terror of Uther coming home, decided to build a tower to hide in if the heir returned. It would be so strong that no man could enter it by force. But however hard the builders worked, each night the earth swallowed up the stones they had laid during the day. Vortigern asked his magicians what to do. They said he must mix its mortar with blood from a son without a father. The wicked king's men searched the land for such a child.

They searched far and wide, until one day they stopped at the gate of a town in Wales. Two little boys were quarreling, one shouting "No father, no father!" at the other – Merlin. He had read Vortigern's mind by his magic and arranged for his friend to let the soldiers know who he was. Merlin told them to take him to the king; he had an important secret to reveal.

The little boy stood before the wicked king and spoke as confidently as a man. The magicians had lied, he said; the reason why the tower could not be built lay beneath its foundations. Two dragons slept deep in a pool under the earth, which moved whenever they did. The magicians laughed at this child who thought he knew more than they did, but the king ordered his men to dig deep down into the mountain-side.

First they found the pool, and the king ordered them to drain it. At the bottom were two chests; when they were opened, two dragons sprang out, one red and one white. At once, they began to fight, breathing fire at each other. At last, the red dragon drove the white one away.

Merlin explained what these wonders meant. The white dragon represented Vortigern and his Saxon friends; the red one Uther Pendragon and the Celtic people of Britain. Uther was now on his way to cast out the usurper. Merlin prophesied that Vortigern would hide, but to no avail; Uther would set fire to his castle, and Vortigern would perish in the flames.

Merlin stood before the wicked king and spoke as confidently as a man.

THE SWORD IN THE STONE

As Merlin foretold, Uther won back his throne. But the new king grew sad and lost courage, when he fell in love with Igrayne, wife of the Duke of Tintagel. Merlin changed the king into Igrayne's husband, and Igrayne had Uther's son, Arthur.

The real duke died in battle, leaving Igrayne free to marry Uther. But they kept Arthur's birth a secret, entrusting him to Merlin, who gave him to a foster father, a knight called Sir Ector. All Igrayne's other children were girls, and when Uther died, there was no prince to succeed him. Merlin prophesied that a new king would be revealed the following Christmas. Uther's lords waited impatiently to see what would happen.

On Christmas Day, the lords went to the greatest church in London, each hoping to be chosen king. To their surprise, a huge stone appeared in the churchyard, with a bright sword plunged into its center. These words were carved on its hilt: "Whosoever pulls out this sword from this stone is rightful king of Britain." Each lord tried the test, but all failed.

Arthur drew the sword out as easily as before. The boy was the rightful king!

By New Year's Day, the king had still not been found. The lords held a tournament while they waited. Knights came from all around to take part; among them Sir Ector, his newly-knighted son Sir Kay, and Kay's foster brother Arthur.

Sir Kay longed to join in the tournament, but he had left his sword at the inn where they were staying. He sent young Arthur to fetch it. As the boy passed the churchyard, he noticed the sword in the stone. Hoping to save time, he pulled the sword. It slipped easily from the stone.

When Arthur returned, the astonished and jealous lords took him straight back to the church and plunged the sword back into the stone. Arthur drew it out again, as easily as before. They had to admit the truth; this lowly boy was their new king! Arthur was made a knight and crowned king on the feast of Pentecost. He held the shining sword Excalibur, forged by magic in another world.

At once, Arthur's kingdom was in danger. The Saxons were back! Arthur rallied his lords to drive the invaders out. His lands secure, Arthur set up court at Camelot and began to rule his kingdom, which he called Logres. His fame spread through all the world. He married Guinevere, daughter of King Leodegraunce, who had helped him in the war. Merlin was uneasy; he knew that Guinevere would one day love another knight.

7

▷ THE ROUND TABLE ◁

Soon Arthur's fame brought trouble. The giant Ryon sent a messenger, demanding Arthur's beard. The giant's cloak was lined with the beards of kings he had defeated. Arthur rode to Ryon's court and killed him.

Another giant was terrorizing the people of an island called St. Michael's Mount. Arthur landed on a rock where an old woman lay weeping. She told him that buried in the rock was a young princess, Elaine, whose nurse she had been. Elaine had died of fear when the giant carried her off. Arthur found the giant roasting stolen pigs on a huge log fire, killed him and took his head back as a trophy to Camelot.

When the giant Ryon challenged Arthur, an old blind harpist asked to carry his standard in the expedition. Arthur refused: "But my friend, you are blind." Suddenly, the harpist changed into a small child. Then he realized that it was Merlin, playing tricks again.

Returning to his usual shape, the magician made a great round table appear in the hall,

Merlin gave the knights the Round Table – symbol of their fellowship.

with seats for many knights. "Here the finest knights of the world will sit," said Merlin. "The table is round to prevent quarrels about precedence." Most of the chairs carried letters of gold: the names of knights who would sit there. But one seat, at the king's right hand, had no name on it yet. "This is the Siege Perilous (Danger Seat), reserved for a particular knight. Any other who dares sit there will die. This knight will achieve a holy quest."

The knights begged Merlin to explain. "When Jesus Christ was crucified, a Roman soldier called Longinus pierced his side with a lance. Joseph of Arimathea, a Roman follower of Christ, caught the blood from this wound in a chalice: the Holy Grail. The descendants of Joseph brought the Grail to Britain, and now it is hidden in a castle. Only he who is to find it may sit in the Siege Perilous."

The knights listened to Merlin in silence. Then, when he had finished his speech, a knight called Gawain spoke. "I vow to go to the aid of any lady who seeks it of this court," he said. "I vow to help any man who asks it of a knight. And I vow to seek any knight who is missing for a year and a day." Each knight repeated Gawain's vows. And thus the order of the Knights of the Round Table was created.

SIR LANCELOT OF THE LAKE

One day, a knight dressed in white asked for hospitality at the gate of a castle called Dolorous Gard. Ten armored knights appeared and barred his way. For two days, he fought them one by one. On the first day, he carried a shield of silver with a red stripe. The second day, his shield had three red stripes and his strength was tripled. Soon, none of the ten was left standing. The people of the castle opened the gates and gave him a triumphant welcome; he had shown that he was the knight who would deliver their castle from a terrible enchantment.

The people then took him to a cemetery. To his horror, he recognized the names on the gravestones: those of knights of the Round Table. At his feet, he saw a marble slab, with an inscription in gold and enamel: "Only the savior of Dolorous Gard may lift this slab; his name is written beneath."

Trembling, the young knight lifted the heavy stone and read the words beneath: "Lancelot of the Lake." At the age of 18, Lancelot had learned his own name!

Lancelot, the son of King Ban and Queen Elaine, had been brought up by the fairy Viviane after his parents were driven out of their kingdom by King Claudas of the Desert Lands. The fairy had brought Lancelot up as if he were her own son. She had never revealed his name, calling him only "sweet child," or "dear foundling." Lancelot knew her only as the Lady of the Lake. The Lady's lands were hidden from human sight under an enchanted lake in a wood. There, Lancelot was educated

to become the best of knights. He learned to read and write, to sing beautifully and play the harp, and to fight bravely in jousts. He was handsome and generous and loved by all.

When he was 18, Lancelot asked the Lady of the Lake: "Madam, please take me to King Arthur's court. It is time that I was dubbed a knight – that is my heart's desire."

The Lady was sad at the thought of losing Lancelot, but proud that he had the qualities to become a great knight. She presented him with a complete set of armor – breastplate, helmet, sword, lance, shield – all shining white, and a white horse. She dressed herself, her knights and pages in white, too, and they rode off to Camelot.

The Lady of the Lake asked for Lancelot to be knighted on the day of Pentecost, when Arthur celebrated his accession. She made him swear to leave Camelot at once to find adventures and never to stay long in one place.

The Lady, who wanted glory for her adopted son, protected him by magic as he traveled. She had given him the magic shield which tripled his strength. True to his promise, he did not stay long at Dolorous Gard, but left as soon as the spell was broken.

Some time later, he went back on another quest. He went into the cellar and found it guarded by two fearsome mechanical knights. With the Lady's magic, he passed them safely and went on to find a chest, in which were the demons that had bewitched the castle. Afterward, he went to the cemetery and found no trace of the graves he had seen before; at last, the castle was completely free. Its name was changed to Joyous Gard, and the grateful people made Lancelot its lord.

News of Lancelot's deeds came regularly to Arthur's court. One day, he passed through Camelot, and the king offered him a place at the Round Table.

Lancelot found the cellar guarded by two fearsome mechanical knights.

▷QUEEN GUINEVERE◁

Arthur held a tournament, so that the court ladies could choose the bravest knights to marry. For two days a forest of banners covered the field. From a richly-painted tent, Queen Guinevere presided over the tournament, surrounded by chattering ladies.

They talked most of all about one knight. The first day he shrank before his opponents and did not win once; but on the next, he astonished them by his bearing and strength. The ladies had eyes only for him. Each secretly hoped to take him for her husband. But he left the tournament without a word. Only Guinevere was happy; she had recognized Lancelot, whom she loved. It was she who had asked him to lose the first day's jousts, as a proof of his love.

Lancelot had fallen in love with the queen when first he arrived at Camelot. Guinevere quickly gave her heart to the handsome young knight, whose exploits were so famous.

Lancelot would do anything for her sake. Many times, he risked his life to save her, but he never revealed his secret love.

Beyond Logres lay the land of Gor, where many of Arthur's subjects were prisoners. But he accepted this as if he was under a spell and did nothing to save them. The King of Gor's son, Meleagant, came to sneer at Arthur. He carried off the queen, hoping to attract Lancelot into his kingdom and kill him. Lancelot set off with Gawain in pursuit of the kidnapper, but he lost his horse when fighting Meleagant, who escaped. Lancelot had lost hope of saving the

Imprisoned by Morgan, Lancelot painted Guinevere's picture on the wall of his cell.

12

Lancelot crossed the Sword Bridge, cutting his hands and feet on its sharp side.

queen, when a dwarf driving a cart offered to take him where he wanted. A cart was a dishonorable thing to ride in – it was used to take criminals to the scaffold. But for love of Guinevere, Lancelot accepted the dwarf's offer and held his head up as he rode.

Two magic bridges led to the castle where Guinevere was imprisoned. Gawain tried the Bridge Under Water and was nearly drowned; and Lancelot tried the Sword Bridge, a huge sword over the dark moat. He crossed it, cutting his hands and feet on its sharp side. Meleagant was waiting, and the two fought furiously. Lancelot won, but spared his rival's life. Guinevere was rescued.

Lancelot's long absences made Guinevere sad. One day, she heard he had entered the land of Morgan Le Fay and thought he was lost forever. Morgan was Arthur's sister, an enchan-

tress who imprisoned faithless lovers in a deep green valley. She did this to revenge herself on a lover who had not been true to her. It was easy to enter the valley, but impossible to leave it, because it was surrounded by an invisible wall.

Morgan had imprisoned hundreds of knights before Lancelot arrived. He could save them because he was a faithful lover who had never betrayed the queen, even in his thoughts. But Morgan, who was not easily beaten, sent two dragons to kill Lancelot, who strangled both. Then three knights in black attacked him. Lancelot used a magic ring, which Guinevere had given him, to make them vanish. The angry enchantress put him into a deep sleep and changed this ring for another, without power. She held Lancelot in prison for a long time. But at last she let him go, for he never forgot Guinevere.

Thinking the knights were angels, Percival knelt down to pray.

In the mountains of Wales, a young hunter saw three shining figures. He thought they were angels and knelt down to pray. Only when they spoke did he realize that they were King Arthur's knights.

Three days later, the boy left his mother. The poor woman's husband and two other sons, all knights, had died in battle. She had tried to keep her last son from this fate, but now he too was off to war. She sadly told him what she knew of a knight's duty. Percival of Wales rode off to be a knight. He knew nothing of the world's ways. Seeing a tent in a meadow, he thought it was a chapel and went in to pray. Inside he found a sleeping lady. He woke her with a kiss and took a ring she wore. His mother had told him never to refuse a kiss or a ring which a lady offered.

This lady was loved by a quarrelsome and jealous knight. He punished her and swore to kill Percival. Percival had made his first enemy.

At last, Percival reached Arthur's court, where he met a knight in scarlet armor riding out. He rode into the great hall, but refused to dismount. When they offered him armor, he said he wanted the scarlet armor of the knight outside. His boldness made a lady laugh. She had been sad and silent for three years. The jealous Sir Kay struck her, then sent Percival to get the scarlet armor – if he could. Percival left the hall, caught the strange knight and killed him with a spear in the eye.

Without knowing it, he had killed one of Arthur's worst enemies. He left his victim's silk shirt and spurs, preferring his own sheepskin coat and whip. But he took his helmet, his lance, his sword and his scarlet shield. Then he vowed to revenge the lady whom Kay had insulted when he arrived.

The first thing he wanted to do, now that he was a knight, was to see his mother again. So he set off westward, but stopped when he saw a sinister castle by the sea. He was met by a beautiful, but sorrowful, lady, called Blanchefleur. She had long been at war with her cousin, Clamadeu of the Isles, and had only 15 knights left to defend her. Next day, Clamadeu would attack again. The lady told Percival that she intended to surrender: "But I will kill myself before I become Clamadeu's prisoner."

Percival swore to help Blanchefleur. He challenged Clamadeu to single combat and beat him, then sent him to Arthur's court, to tell Kay that Percival intended to avenge the insult to the lady he had slapped.

Percival wanted to stay with Blanchefleur, but he remembered his mother and left. As he rode on, he met a thin, ragged lady riding a skinny horse. It was the lady he had kissed when he set out for Arthur's court! She had been mistreated by the jealous knight she loved. Percival fought the knight and soon held him at his mercy. Another prisoner went to pay homage at Arthur's court.

Winter had come, and snow covered the ground. Percival saw three drops of blood on the earth. He dismounted and fell asleep, dreaming of Blanchefleur's scarlet lips and white skin. Sagremor the Unruly, one of a group of Arthur's knights who were resting nearby, found him lying beside his horse. Sagremor, who got his name for his sudden rages, attacked Percival; before he knew what had hit him, he landed head first in the snow. Percival returned to his dreams. Back at the camp, Sir Kay mocked Sagremor. Arthur sent him to find the strange sleeping knight. Kay soon returned with a broken collarbone. Percival had repaid his insult to a lady.

Percival continued his journey home, but was sad to learn that his mother was dead, heart-broken at the loss of her youngest son. Percival decided to stay with Arthur and became one of his most famous knights.

THE HOLY GRAIL

One day, Percival found himself by a river too wide to cross. There was no bridge or ford, so he started to turn back. Then he saw a boat with two fishermen in it. They invited Percival on board and took him to a castle deep in the forest. "This is the castle of Carbonek," said one. "I am its king. I cannot ride because I have a wound which will not heal. So I go fishing to distract myself."

Then the fisher-king invited Percival to a feast. Before each course was served, a strange procession crossed the hall. First came a page carrying a shining lance whose point dripped blood, then two boys carrying golden candle-sticks. Then, bathed in bright light, came a lady carrying a vase of pure gold set with jewels, followed by another carrying a silver dish.

Percival asked no questions. His mother had always told him not to be curious. Next morning he found the castle deserted, but his armor and horse ready for him. He understood he must leave this strange place.

Back at the Round Table, Percival thought no more of Carbonek. A feast was held in his honor, and on its third day, an ugly lady rode in on a mule, asking to be heard by the king and

Young Percival was a very religious knight.

his companions. Her skin was yellow as her mule's. She reproached Percival for not questioning the fisher-king about the mysterious procession. He had seen the Holy Grail without knowing it.

Percival swore to return to Carbonek for the Grail. Then 15 knights swore to follow him. The quest of the Grail had begun.

For many years, Percival wandered through the kingdom, without finding the road to Carbonek. One day he rescued two knights who were hanging by their feet from a tree. Sir Kay, the malicious steward, had put them there. Percival went on and met several knights coming down a hill. They had all gone mad! He recognized some from the Round Table. A woman rode quickly past, crying: "Take care, Sire. Don't go up the hill, for you may lose your reason or your life!"

But Percival rode on up the hill. At the top he

The Grail procession entered the great hall.

found a stone column, so tall he could not see its top. All around were lines of smaller stones. He dismounted and tied his horse to the main column and laid down his shield and helmet. Then a young girl appeared. She told him he had tied his horse to a magic column, which Merlin had made. Only a perfect knight could touch the column without going mad. She showed Percival the road to Carbonek, then disappeared.

Percival was recognized and welcomed by the people of the castle. As before he saw the Grail procession, but this time he asked his host what it meant. "You shall know," said the king, "if you can put the pieces of this broken sword back together." Percival did so. At last he could learn the secret of Carbonek.

The fisher-king was the keeper of the lance which had pierced Christ's side, and the vase in which his blood had been caught. But the king had been wounded and could not carry out his tasks properly, so the kingdom had fallen under a spell. Percival could heal the king by avenging his brother, murdered by a cruel knight called Pertinax. Percival confronted him in his tower. At the moment when Percival cut off Pertinax's head, the fisher-king's wound was healed.

Percival told Arthur his adventures, but without mentioning the Grail. He asked to sit at the Siege Perilous. Arthur tried to stop him; six knights who had tried to sit there had been swallowed up by the earth. Without a word, Percival pushed past the knights who tried to bar his way and sat in the Siege Perilous. The earth opened up – and out came the six knights who had been swallowed. Merlin's prophecy had come true.

Percival married his beloved Blanchefleur and later succeeded the fisher-king. But he missed his adventurous life.

17

THE STORMY FOUNTAIN

Sir Calogrenant was telling the others how his pride had led to a fall. King Arthur dozed, but his nephew Yvain did not miss a word. "Once, in the forest of Broceliande, I met a hunchback. He told me of an enchanted fountain, whose water boiled, though cold as stone. It stood under a pine tree, from which hung a golden bowl. By the fountain lay a huge emerald, set with four bright rubies. 'If you put water in the bowl and pour it over the stone,' he said, 'You

18

The marriage of Yvain and the Lady Laudine.

will unleash a terrible storm. It will bring you a chance to win great honor.' "

The knight went on, "I found the fountain and did what the hunchback suggested. At once there was thunder and lightning; the terrified animals fled. At last, when the storm died down, I heard beautiful music; in the tree were thousands of singing birds. Then, suddenly, a knight attacked me. My lance broke against his shield, I fell to the ground and he took my horse and rode off, to my great shame."

Yvain longed to try the same quest. Cruel Sir Kay teased him. This was a quest for a knight like him or Gawain, not an untried squire. Arthur, waking, said he would go to the fountain himself, in two week's time.

Yvain secretly got his armor and horse ready. He rode off to the forest, where he easily found the fountain and unleashed the storm. The mysterious, angry knight rode in, wearing black armor. The forest rang with their weapons. Even when their lances were broken they fought on. At last, Yvain lifted his enemy's helmet with his sword.

Mortally wounded, the black knight fled to his castle. Yvain, wanting proof of his deed, followed. As he entered the castle, a heavy gate fell behind him. Another closed in front; he was a prisoner!

A dark passage led to a richly painted chamber. There Yvain met a lady, beautiful as moonlight. "I am Luned," she said. "You have killed my mistress's lord. His angry followers are after you. But I shall help you, Squire Yvain; you alone did not scorn me when I came to Arthur's court one day."

Luned gave Yvain a ring which made him invisible. He sat quietly while his pursuers ran by. She dressed his wounds, gave him clothing and brought him food.

Next day Yvain saw a lady in the garden. Though she looked very sad, she was very beautiful. At once he fell in love and asked Luned who she was. She was the Lady Laudine, whose husband he had killed. He loved a lady who must hate him!

19

Yvain and the lion kill a giant.

THE KNIGHT OF THE LION

Seeing how sad Yvain was, Luned tried to help. Day after day she encouraged Laudine to remarry. The fountain must have a new guardian. And who better to protect it than he who killed the last guardian? It worked: when Laudine met Yvain and saw how much he loved her, she agreed to become his wife.

The marriage feast was drawing to a close when the fountain let out its storm again. Yvain went to fight whoever had started it. It was King Arthur, come to try the test, as he had said he would a fortnight before. His best knights were there, too. Sir Kay won the honor of fighting the fountain's guardian. None of them recognized Yvain, who easily beat the malicious steward.

Yvain told them who he was and invited them to stay. As they left, the knights insisted he come too: "Only an idle knight deserts his work for a woman's love!" said Gawain. Yvain let them persuade him. He said farewell to Laudine, promising to return the next year. She gave him a magic ring to protect him – so long as he stayed faithful to her.

Yvain went back with Gawain, and the two formed a team at tournaments. Yvain enjoyed the sport so much that he forgot his promise to his wife. One day, a lady came to him: "I come from the Lady Laudine," she told Yvain. "You have betrayed her. She has almost died of grief. She forbids you to come back and asks you to return the ring she gave you."

Yvain went mad with grief. He tore his clothes, scratched his face and wandered aimlessly through the deep forest. He might have starved to death, except for the charity of a hermit who gave him bread and water.

At last, a lady cousin found him asleep under a tree and rubbed him with a magic ointment, which restored his sanity. At her castle, she nursed him back to health. When he was well, he thanked her by fighting her greatest enemy. The lady wanted to marry Yvain, but he returned to wandering.

As he crossed a dark forest, Yvain heard a painful roar. A lion was in the clutches of a fire-breathing snake. Yvain went to the lion's aid, hiding behind his shield to keep himself from the flames. He cut off part of the snake's tail and drove it away.

Yvain and the lion became inseparable. They hunted together, ate the same food and at night slept huddled together for warmth.

One day, they reached the stormy fountain. Yvain sadly thought of his lost wife. He heard a voice from a nearby chapel – Luned! Falsely accused of treachery by a wicked knight she would be burned to death the next day, unless a champion came to her defense. Yvain offered to challenge the knight and his brothers. They laughed at him – until they saw the lion. Yvain and the lion put the traitors out of action.

Laudine came to congratulate the winner, not recognizing her husband. She wished him good luck in love. Yvain felt very sad.

Yvain became the defender of any lady who needed help. Only Luned knew who he was, keeping his secret faithfully. He grew famous as the Knight of the Lion. The lion and he killed a giant who had captured four knights and rescued some poor girls from a demon who had made them slaves. Soon Laudine was ready to marry again. Cunning Luned said the famous Knight of the Lion would be a good guardian of the stormy fountain.

One day the storm broke, so Laudine went to see who had disturbed the fountain. It was the Knight of the Lion! She was amazed to learn who he was. At last, she forgave Yvain. They walked home hand in hand.

The King, delighted by the young musician's company, asked him to stay.

THE DEEDS OF TRISTAN

King Mark of Cornwall's sister died giving birth to a son. Her husband Rivalen named him Tristan, which means "sad," and sent him to be brought up by his marshal Roualt and a trusted groom, Gorneval. Fifteen years later, Rivalen was killed by his enemy, Duke Morgan. Roualt thought the best way to protect Tristan from the wicked duke was to send him to his uncle Mark at Tintagel Castle.

Tristan and his uncle had never met. The boy

wanted to win a place at court by his own worth, not by being the king's nephew. So he dressed as a wandering minstrel with a harp on his back. The king, delighted by the young musician's company, asked him to stay. One day Tristan felt a sad atmosphere in the king's great hall. All the women were crying, and even the men could hardly hold back their tears. A cold-eyed, grim-faced giant confronted the king. It was Morholt, the king of Ireland's brother-in-law.

Morholt had come to claim tribute of 300 young men and 300 young ladies, which Mark had to pay the Irish king after losing a war. This cruel treaty would end if Morholt was beaten in single combat, but no champion was brave enough to challenge the giant.

Tristan asked to fight Morholt, but first he had to reveal his true identity. The champion had to be of noble birth. All at once King Mark felt joy at finding his nephew, and fear of losing him forever.

Tristan and Morholt fought alone on an island with knives and swords. Tristan could not avoid Morholt's knife, which pierced his thigh; but he planted the point of his sword in the giant's skull. The giant was mortally wounded. Tristan's sword broke as Morholt fell, leaving a piece of metal in his wound.

Tristan barely had the strength to return to Tintagel, where he fell down in a swoon, among the rejoicing people. For days he lay twisting with pain, his body swollen and blackened. Morholt had poisoned his knife.

Mark's doctors could not heal Tristan. He said farewell to his uncle and asked to be cast away at the mercy of the tides, in a boat without sails or oars. Legends said that this way he would reach a magic land, where fairies would cure him. All he took was his harp, which he played to soothe his pain.

After drifting for days, Tristan landed on the Irish coast. Some fishermen found him and took him to the king's castle. They knew the queen could heal him with magic herbs. But Tristan was afraid to meet the queen – the sister of Morholt, whom he had killed. His illness had made him look different, so he said he was Tantris, a minstrel, the only survivor of a shipwreck.

The Queen's golden-haired daughter Iseult, who was beautiful and kind, took great care of him. As he grew well, Tristan taught her songs from his own country. But at last he decided to return to Cornwall, in case Morholt's friends recognized him.

Glad to see his nephew again, King Mark made Tristan his heir. Some lords grew jealous and pressed the king to marry again and have a son. Mark did not want to marry. But he had to do what his lords wanted, in case they turned against him. The day came for his answer. As the lords settled in Mark's hall, two swallows flew in from the sea and dropped a long lock of golden hair on Mark's shoulder. Playing for time, Mark said he would marry only the woman whose hair it was. Tristan thought of fair Iseult. He sailed next day for Ireland.

Dying, Tristan sailed off in an open boat at the mercy of the tides.

TRISTAN AND ISEULT

Tristan and his friends landed at Wexford, where they heard a cruel dragon was at large. The king had promised Iseult's hand in marriage to whoever killed it. Tristan fought the monster, killed it, then cut out its tongue and hid it in his shoe, as proof of victory. But going back, he collapsed. The dragon's tongue was poisonous.

While Tristan lay unconscious, the king's steward passed by and found the monster's body. He cut off its head and galloped to the

Tristan and the dragon of Wexford.

castle to claim Iseult's hand. He had loved her for a long time. Iseult, who did not want to marry him, sensed deception. She went and found the sick Tristan, whom she did not recognize as the "musician" she had nursed before. Once again, Iseult and the queen nursed him for several days.

One day, cleaning Tristan's sword, Iseult noticed its blade was broken. She looked at it for a while, then went to a box, where she kept the piece of metal taken from Morholt's skull. It fitted Tristan's sword perfectly. This man had killed her uncle – but he alone could prove the steward a liar!

Her mother advised Iseult to spare him. But, when he asked for her hand on King Mark's behalf, Iseult was upset. The queen, wanting her daughter to be happily married, gave a servant a magic potion. A couple who shared it would love each other until death.

As they sailed to Cornwall, Tristan tried to console the unhappy girl. One hot day, they asked the wicked servant for a drink. She put the queen's love potion in the cup they shared. It did its work; Tristan and Iseult fell passionately in love.

Tristan dared not tell his uncle, and the marriage took place as arranged. But each day, he met Iseult secretly by a shady fountain in the castle ground. Sometimes he went to her chamber, taking great care not to be discovered. But the jealous lords were spying and told King Mark. He found the lovers together and ordered them to be burned to death, without trial.

A sad crowd gathered on the road to the stake. As he passed a chapel on the cliff top, Tristan asked to go in and pray. His jailers untied his hands, and he ran off and jumped over the cliff. He landed on a ledge, miraculously unhurt, and jumped down to the beach. Gorneval, his groom, waited there with his sword and horse. Tristan rode back and carried off Iseult.

For three years, the couple hid in the forest. But, eventually, King Mark discovered their hiding place. He found the couple asleep in their little hut. They were both so thin that he took pity on them and said that Iseult would be welcomed back to his court. But Tristan must go into exile.

Tristan tried to hide near his love, but spies found him again. At last, he departed for Armorique, on the coast of France.

There Tristan went to the king's court and quickly became friends with the king's son, Kaherdin. Kaherdin's sister was another Iseult: Iseult of the White Hands. Tristan thought he might be able to get over his fair Iseult by marrying her. But he never forgot his first love. His wife and her brother realized his heart was not his own.

Tristan was badly wounded one day, saving his friend from a jealous dwarf. Afraid he was dying, he asked Kaherdin to fetch fair Iseult from Cornwall. Only she could cure him. When Kaherdin set off, he promised to use a white sail if Iseult was returning with him, a black one if she was not.

But Tristan's wife, Iseult of the White Hands, had overheard them. In a jealous rage, she told Tristan, too weak to look out of the window, that she saw the ship with a black sail. Thinking Iseult had deserted him, Tristan died of grief. When fair Iseult saw his body, she wept and died, too.

The lovers were buried side by side. Mark planted a rose on Iseult's grave and a vine on Tristan's. They grew tangled together, as if to show that love is stronger than death.

The lovers were united at last.

Merlin taught Viviane how to enchant him.

MERLIN AND VIVIANE

What became of the great enchanter, Merlin? After leading Arthur's army against the Saxons, bringing the Round Table to Camelot and presiding over the birth or marriage of many knights, he seemed to disappear.

Merlin loved to travel, sometimes in disguise. Once, as he walked through the mysterious forest of Broceliande in the shape of a handsome young squire, he saw a young girl admiring herself in the water of a lake. She was the fairy Viviane – the Lady of the Lake. Merlin fell in love with her and tried to win her with enchantments, making a magnificent castle appear and then disappear again.

From that day on, the enchanter was often absent from Arthur's court. He would go to meet Viviane in secret. To keep her love, he taught her some of his own magic spells. The girl learned to dance on water without getting wet and to make a spring rise up whenever she wanted.

Viviane wanted to keep Merlin by her side forever. She wheedled all his secrets from him. Then, as he slept, she made a magic circle around him. He was her prisoner forever after. He had returned forever into the other world, that of the fairies and magicians. He did not mind, for he loved Viviane more than liberty.

Turpin

Charlemagne

Naismes

Huon

Roland

Oliver

CHARLEMAGNE

Unlike King Arthur, who may or may not have existed, Charlemagne was without doubt a real person. He was the first Holy Roman Emperor. Even so, he is the subject of many legends. Medieval French poets wrote *chansons de geste* about his knights and their deeds. These long poems are set in a magical land very different from the real Europe of the early Middle Ages.

Charlemagne was the son of Pepin the Short, King of the Franks, and his wife Berthe. Legend says that Berthe was kidnapped on the way to marry Pepin, who had never met her, and a wicked servant, Aliste, took her place. Aliste became a proud and greedy queen, hated by her people. But one day, Berthe's mother came to court and unmasked the false queen. Pepin found the real Berthe living in a forest. Their first son, Charles, became known as Charlemagne – "Great Charles."

Aliste's wicked sons poisoned Pepin and Berthe and tried to murder Charles. But he escaped and hid in Toledo, in Spain, which was then a Moslem city. Years later, Galafre, the Emir of Toledo, made him a knight, while fighting a war against a rival emir. Charles used his magical sword, Joyeuse, to kill the enemy emir. The sword was a gift from Galienne, the emir's daughter, who was betrothed to Charles.

Galienne found out by looking in a magic mirror that her jealous brother, Marsile, was plotting against Charles. Charles exposed the traitor, married Galienne and went back to reclaim his kingdom of France. He drove out his half-brothers and took the crown. But his joy turned to sadness when Galienne died.

Charlemagne got his name from his great height. He had a terrible temper and was very strong. He was believed to be able to lift up a knight in armor and

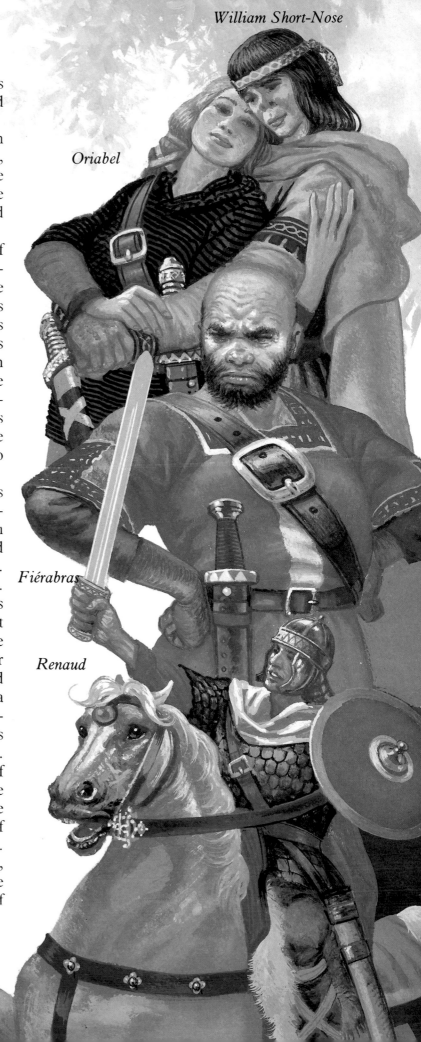

Oriabel

Fiérabras

Renaud

to break horseshoes with his bare hands. His shining armor lit up the dark night, and criminals fell dead when he approached.

His palace at Aix-la-Chapelle (modern Aachen) was the finest in Christendom. There, he sat on a throne of gold and ivory. The chapel, it is said, was made bigger by a miracle when it proved too small. It is also said that God gave the emperor the city's hot springs.

Charlemagne, the greatest Christian ruler of his time, fought ceaselessly against two particular enemies: the Moslem Saracens and the pagan Saxons, who worshipped many gods including Odin and Thor. There are legends about his wars. One says that St. James appeared to the emperor one night and told him how to follow the Milky Way to free the pilgrims' roads to the saint's shrine at Compostella, in Spain, then held by Moslems. The walls of Pamplona fell down miraculously when he besieged it. A miraculous white stag is said to have guided his army into Italy.

Some of Charlemagne's knights in the stories were real people, some imaginary. They included Roland, his nephew in legend, but in reality, the Prefect of Brittany, who died heroically at Roncevaux, on August 15, AD 778. Roland's great friend Oliver is imaginary. Bishop Turpin, who would exchange his cross for a sword when necessary, also died at Roncevaux, after giving his companions the Last Rites. Charlemagne had a wise counselor named Naismes de Bavière, who often calmed his terrible rages. Huon de Bordeaux is a legendary knight, whose adventures were inspired by the wars of the early French kings against the independent lords of Aquitaine. William Short-Nose was inspired by William of Toulouse, who drove the Moslems from the Narbonne region in AD 793. Saracen knights are often shown in the stories as giants; one of them, Fiérabras, joined Charlemagne's army. Renaud, with his wonderful horse Bayart, appears in one of the most popular poems of the Middle Ages, the story of the Four Sons of Aymes.

OGIER THE DANE

Ogier the Dane, a knight of Charlemagne's, saw his son, Beaudounet, and the emperor's son, Charlot, quarrel. Charlot, a bad loser, threw his chessboard at Beaudounet's head. Ogier saw his son fall down dead. When Charlemagne refused to punish his own son, Ogier declared himself free of his vows to him. He swore to kill the murderer with his own hand.

Ogier fled to Italy and sought the help of the King of Lombardy. Charlemagne pursued him with his army. Ogier's horse, Briefort, saved his life, galloping across the emperor's ranks and down a Roman road to Tuscany.

Ogier defended a fortress alone against Charlemagne's army for seven years, with wooden knights on the battlements to deceive them. But at last, he had to surrender.

Charlemagne ordered his prisoner to be put on low rations. Ogier, almost a giant, had a vast appetite; he could not live on crusts of bread and water. Bishop Turpin secretly sent him extra food every day: 50 loaves, a quarter of an ox, and a huge cask of wine.

The others thought Ogier dead. A Saracen leader, Brehus, saw his chance to invade the Frankish kingdom. Charlemagne wept, wishing he could call the brave but rebellious Dane. Then Turpin revealed that Ogier was alive.

Ogier was freed to fight Brehus. He asked leave, in exchange, to punish his son's killer. But as he was about to strike Charlot, an angel stopped his hand. Ogier fetched Briefort, the only horse who could carry him, and rode off to kill the Saracen.

Oliver fought the giant Fiérabras by the walls of Rome.

Oliver, the King of Vienna's nephew, was famous for his courtesy. His uncle rebelled against Charlemagne, who besieged the city. As time passed, his young knights grew bored and held a tournament. From the ramparts, Oliver saw them jousting. He was bored, too. Oliver took his helmet and slipped out of the city to join the jousters on the other side. Toppling their wooden targets, he cried "Up with Vienna!" and rode off.

Roland, the emperor's nephew, chased him to the gate and challenged him. They were worthy foes, of equal strength, and they fought until sunset. Neither won outright. "We should have been friends," they said.

Suddenly, a shining cloud came down. In its center, the young men saw the angel Gabriel· "God needs your valor," he said. "He will call you soon to Spain to fight the Moslems. Make friends, now!" The two went back and persuaded their uncles to make peace.

Years later, Charlemagne went to save Rome from Saracens who had pillaged the Holy City, killed the Pope and massacred the citizens. From the cathedral, they stole casks of a miraculous ointment which was said to have cured Christ's wounds on the Cross.

The Saracens found they could not be injured if they used the ointment. Many of Charlemagne's knights were hurt. The Saracen giant Fiérabras challenged them all. Oliver, badly wounded, took up the challenge.

Oliver courteously helped his foe get ready. The giant offered the sacred ointment to cure his wounds. Oliver refused, despite the pain. But, when near the casks, he tipped them into the Tiber. Fighting on equal terms, he won.

Fiérabras became a Christian and joined the Franks. Every year, on St. John's·Day, the casks floated to the top of the river.

▷ YOUNG ROLAND ◁

Roland was born in a dark forest in Italy. His mother Berthe, Charlemagne's sister, had married a poor knight, Milon, against the emperor's wishes. The couple rode off to Rome, to beg the Pope to ask Charlemagne's forgiveness. But bandits robbed them, and they had to go on foot. In Rome, they sadly heard the Pope had taken Charlemagne's side.

Roland was born as they made their way back, near the town of Sutri, where they went to live in a cave. Twelve years later, Charlemagne stopped at Sutri and invited the people to dine at his camp. Young Roland sat near the emperor and ate greedily – then stuffed his shirt with meat and bread for his parents.

The curious emperor sent soldiers to find out who the hungry boy was, and so Berthe and Milon were found. Charlemagne forgave them for Roland's sake and took the boy to court to learn to be a knight.

Roland was a bright boy, impatient for battle. Just 15 years old, he ran away to join his uncle's war against the Saracens. On the way, he recruited other boys: riding farm horses, armed with sticks and stones, they arrived at the turning point of a battle.

Charlemagne had been captured by the giant Eaumont, who took his helmet. The emperor was at his mercy. Then up rode an unknown youth, who knocked off the Saracen's head with a crowbar. The emperor recognized his nephew. Realizing it was time to make him a knight, he gave him Eaumont's magic sword. Its name was carved on the blade: Durandel.

Soon Roland's deeds and courage were

Young Roland sat near the Emperor and ate greedily.

known all over the land. But his character was not so admirable. Once his uncle put him in the ranks as a punishment. Instead of accepting his penalty, Roland deserted with his friends to capture a town in Spain. By doing this, he had placed the Franks' victory at risk. His angry uncle struck him. Upset, Roland sailed east to offer his services to the King of Persia, who sent him to rescue a princess. On his return he fell in tears at Charlemagne's feet, begging for his pardon.

Pride was Roland's undoing. Charlemagne had accepted the Emir Marsile's offer of peace. Roland wanted to go on fighting. But the other knights, tired of battle, wanted to go home. Ganelon, the knight whom Berthe had married when Milon died, called his stepson an arrogant fool. Roland told Ganelon to take Charle-

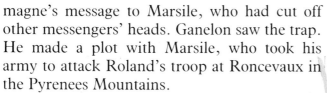

magne's message to Marsile, who had cut off other messengers' heads. Ganelon saw the trap. He made a plot with Marsile, who took his army to attack Roland's troop at Roncevaux in the Pyrenees Mountains.

Roland's troop, few in number and taken by surprise, were defeated. But Roland refused to blow his horn to call Charlemagne's army back. By his side, all the best knights fell: Bishop Turpin and Oliver, his friend. The dying Roland, with his last breath, put the horn to his

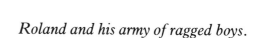

Roland and his army of ragged boys.

mouth and blew three times.

Charlemagne reached the site of battle too late. He wept to see so many young knights dead. By Roland's body was a shattered rock; he had tried to break his magic sword on it, to keep it out of enemy hands. But the rock had broken instead! The next day, the sun was hung with shadows; storms broke and the earth tore itself open. Was God announcing the death of his knight Roland?

MISSION IMPOSSIBLE

Three times, the hunchbacked dwarf Auberon, king of the dark fairy forest, had greeted Huon with great courtesy. Three times, the young man had not responded. The angry dwarf raised tempests and tore up the trees like grass. But none of Huon's knights returned his greeting. Gériaume, their hermit guide, had warned them; anyone who spoke to Auberon would be his prisoner for eternity.

But Huon could not believe that the dwarf wished him ill. Had he not always offered help? Huon had great need of help. He thought as he rode of his sad plight. Once one of Charlemagne's knights, now he was exiled, unjustly driven out of France.

It had happened very quickly. Why had Charlot, Charlemagne's son, attacked Huon and his brother Gerard? Gerard was wounded, so Huon had rushed to his defense – and killed the emperor's son before he knew him. Blinded by grief, the emperor could not admit Huon's innocence. He took away his lands in Bordeaux and sent him to certain death, by giving him an impossible task.

Huon had to capture the city of Babylon after crossing the perilous Red Sea. Then he must enter the palace of King Gaudisse, cut off the head of the first Saracen at his table, steal three kisses from Esclarmonde, Gaudisse's beautiful daughter, and exact tribute of 1000 bears, 1000 hounds, 1000 young knights and 1000 beautiful

Auberon's anger unleashed a great storm.

maidens. And, as if this were not enough, Huon must bring Charlemagne Gaudisse's moustache and four of his teeth! Only then could he go home and reclaim his lands.. But how could he hope to survive when only 11 brave knights had agreed to come with him on this adventure?

The knights went to Rome, then to Brindisi, from where they crossed the Mediterranean Sea. After a pilgrimage to Jerusalem, they crossed enchanted lands: Ferminia, where the sun never shone, and the land of the Koumans, hairy creatures which ate raw meat. Then they met the hermit Gériaume, an exiled Frankish knight, who offered to guide them. First, they must cross a magic forest.

Auberon's offer of help was welcome – why not accept it? Next time the dwarf appeared, Huon spoke: "Sire, you are most welcome." To everyone's great relief, Auberon smiled.

Auberon took the hungry knights to his palace for a delicious supper. He told them he was the son of Julius Caesar and the fairy Morgan. At his birth, the fairies had given him

many gifts: he could read people's thoughts, travel instantly wherever he wanted and tame even the wildest animals. But one ill-wishing fairy had made him a hunchbacked dwarf – though she had sweetened the curse by giving him a beautiful face.

Before Huon left, Auberon offered him two magic gifts: a cask which filled itself with wine, and an ivory horn. This made the sick well and the sad happy; anyone who heard it would start singing. No matter where the horn was blown, Auberon would hear it, so that Huon could call the dwarf to his aid. But woe to him if he ever told a lie or blew the horn except in direst need!

Huon and his band said goodbye to Auberon and set out across the Saracen lands – where every Christian was in mortal danger.

Huon crossed the land of the Koumans.

35

Huon crossed the Red Sea on the back of a monster.

36

Huon would not be prudent, despite the old hermit's advice. The emperor's forgiveness was more important than his own safety.

In his hasty fashion, he went to save the city of Tormont from its ruler Eudes, a Frankish knight who had become a Moslem. He was cruel to the Christians who lived there. Huon deliberately made Eudes angry by giving free drinks to the poor Christians from his magic cask; then when Eudes came for him, he blew the ivory horn. Auberon arrived with an army and drove the tyrant away.

Auberon summoned a sea monster to take Huon across the Red Sea but forbade him to go to a castle on its other shore, built by his father Julius Caesar. Giant Arrogance, who lived there, had robbed Auberon of a magic coat of mail which protected its wearer from wounds, flood and fire.

"That'll do for me!" answered Huon. "I didn't leave France for a dull life. I'll win the magic coat." The dwarf was angry: "In that case, my friend, blow my horn all you like; I'll never rescue you again."

Giant Arrogance's castle was guarded by two fearsome brass men. Strange machinery made them move. Each swung a deadly ball and chain. No creature could pass unscathed.

A golden bowl hung from a pillar. Huon hit it with his sword. The castle echoed with the noise. Not even this woke the giant, asleep inside. Sebille, a captive princess, saw Huon and opened a grating in the tower. The mechanical men stood still. Inside, Sebille showed Huon the giant's room. He woke him up and challenged him to fight.

The giant fought with a scythe. He was the most terrifying figure Huon had ever seen: 17 feet tall, with eyes that glowed like coals. Luckily, Huon found the magic coat and put it on. The giant threw his scythe straight at him, but it turned away and stuck in a pillar. The weaponless giant fled, tripping over a club which Sebille had dropped. Huon cut his head off. From the giant's hand he took a ring, which King Gaudisse had given him as a sign of loyalty. Then Huon set off for Babylon.

To reach Gaudisse's palace, Huon had to cross four bridges, with a guard on each. "Are you a Moslem?" asked the first. Huon said, "Yes," in order to pass; but realized his mistake. Auberon had said that if he lied, he would not be his friend. Huon showed the other guards the giant's ring; they thought Arrogance had sent him and let him pass.

Huon entered Gaudisse's hall. The Saracens watched horrified as he cut off the first one's head. He saw the lovely Esclarmonde and kissed her three times. The princess fainted with shock.

Gaudisse's guards captured Huon, but let him go when they saw the gold ring. "What news of Arrogance?" asked the king. Huon dared not lie again and admitted killing the giant. He was led to a dungeon.

Hasty Huon seemed to have failed, just on the point of success. But Gériaume and his friends came to the rescue. And Esclarmonde, who had fallen in love when Huon kissed her, joined in on his side. Huon killed Gaudisse, took his moustache and four teeth, and set off home. He had many adventures on his way. He killed Giant Arrogance's brother, who attacked him for revenge. Pirates captured Esclarmonde and sold her as a slave. Huon fought 3000 Saracens to rescue her.

In Rome, Esclarmonde was baptized as a Christian. Huon and she were married, but their troubles were not over. At home, Huon had been falsely accused of a crime. The emperor had ordered his execution. But Auberon quelled Charlemagne's rage. Thanks to the fairy king, Huon and Charlemagne were friends again and remained so forever.

Renaud, son of Duke Aymes of Dordone, killed the emperor's nephew, Bertolais, in a quarrel over a game of chess. Bertolais had called Renaud a cheat and a liar, and hit him. Renaud restrained himself from hitting back and asked Charlemagne for justice. But the emperor teased him. The enraged young knight hit his rival with the heavy chessboard, killing him instantly. The emperor wanted to hang Renaud there and then, but in the confusion the young knight escaped with his brothers, Aalard, Guichard and Richard. Charlemagne had made them knights only the day before – and already they were banished!

They rode off toward Dordone. Renaud rode Bayart, a magnificent bay the emperor had given him – a wonderful horse which understood human speech. When the others' horses fell down exhausted, Bayart took all four on his back without slowing down.

But there was no welcome for them at home. Their father disowned them and threatened to give them up. So they were forced to wander with their 300 followers. They searched the dark Ardennes forest for refuge and came to the river Meuse, which fell in a torrent down the mountains. "Let's build a fortress up there," exclaimed Renaud. They called it Montessor. High on a rocky slope, it was impregnable.

For seven years, the brothers lived there quietly. Charlemagne lost their trail. But one fine day, out hunting, Aalard, Guichard and Richard met a troop of knights – the advance guard of the emperor's army. The brothers attacked the party, killed its leader and took their mules, loaded with gold, silver and precious fabrics.

Charlemagne was angry. Renaud had flouted him! In broad daylight, he had ridden Bayart into the camp and carried off a jewel from the top of the emperor's tent. The emperor was ready to strike camp when a knight called Hervis de Lausanne offered to slip into Montessor with a band of armed men.

Hervis went to the fortress gate and told the brothers he was disgusted by the war and by Charlemagne's injustice. He asked to join their side. They trusted the traitor and welcomed him in. But late that night, he let his soldiers into the castle; the brothers just managed to flee through a secret passage.

With Charlemagne in hot pursuit, they hid in the forest. The emperor gave up at the Espaux Gorge, a fearful place, haunted by fairies who played tricks on unwary travelers.

Chilly winter came. The brothers lived on roots, which made them and the horses ill. Only Bayart seemed better than ever. His coat shone. The brothers headed back to Dordone, hoping not to be recognized in their thin and dirty state. Again, they all rode on Bayart's back.

When the duchess saw the four worn-out travelers, she knew her sons at once. She took care of them and gave them gold. Renaud suggested going to Spain to fight the Saracens. They set off with 700 knights. Fearful of ambushes, one day they heard the rattle of a chariot. Soon a knight appeared, followed by a troop of armed men. Slowly, as he approached, the driver's face became clear. Renaud broke into laughter; it was their cousin Maugis – knight, magician and highwayman!

MAUGIS, THE MAGICIAN

Maugis's fairy godmother, Oriande, had given him many gifts. He could see in the dark, cross huge distances instantly and hear the slightest noise. He could make magic potions from herbs. By magic, he lured rich lords to his castle and robbed them. "I'll come with you!" he cried to the brothers. "Look at the gold and jewels I've tricked out of Charlemagne!"

Bayart took all four brothers on his strong back.

39

Together with Maugis, the four rode south to Bordeaux, where King Yon of Gascony was under Saracen attack. Why not fight here instead of in Spain? Renaud captured Bègue, the Saracen commander. As he did so, Bayart grasped the Saracen's horse by its mane and proudly led his captive to his master.

The grateful king let the brothers build a fortress on his land. They chose a high plain over the Dordogne and built Montauban, a marble castle. Renaud married Clarisse, the king's sister.

Charlemagne brooded angrily; more than ever, he wanted them hanged. Roland offered to catch them, but he needed a horse as good as Bayart. The emperor announced a race; Roland would take the winning horse, whose owner would receive 400 gold marks, 100 silk shirts and Charlemagne's crown.

On the day of the race, a squire rode in on a lame white horse. The other riders laughed, but on the track, his horse left them standing. Spurning the other prizes, the young man galloped away with the crown. Charlemagne recognized Renaud and Bayart, magically disguised by Maugis.

Enraged, the emperor ordered King Yon to give them up or have his head shaved and ears clipped. Under threat, Yon betrayed his friends. Alone and unarmed, the brothers set out for what they thought were peace talks.

On the way, Ogier the Dane had set an ambush. In a rocky, wooded valley, between four streams, a thousand knights hid on each side. Fording the River Vaupaire, Renaud discovered the trap; too late! The brothers fought for their lives. Renaud's thigh was wounded and Richard's chest cut open. There was no hope for them. If only they had brought Bayart and Maugis.

But suddenly, they saw Ogier's men flee. Maugis had come to the rescue, having sent the men at Charlemagne's camp to sleep. He healed Renaud and Richard by rubbing their wounds with magic herbs.

Many times Charlemagne scented victory, but the cunning brothers always slipped away. One day Richard was captured and led to the gallows. When his brothers did not come, he thought they had deserted him. They were asleep, tired out. But Bayart heard Richard's cries and drummed his hooves to wake them. They ran to Richard's aid and cut the rope from his neck!

The brothers decided to force Charlemagne to make peace. As the emperor slept, Maugis flew him by magic to Montauban, where he woke, surrounded by his enemies. He thought his time was up, but Renaud, who respected him too much to kill him, set him free.

The stubborn emperor, far from making peace, besieged Montauban. Soon everyone in the fortress was starving. Old Duke Aymes took pity and shot hams over the wall with a catapult. But it was not enough to feed so many people. Clarisse begged Renaud to surrender. Their two sons were near death.

The knights resigned themselves to eating their horses. But when Bayart's turn came Renaud refused to kill his friend. Instead, he cut into Bayart's veins and gave his sons the blood to drink. Bayart, tough as he was, wasted away visibly; but he willingly gave his blood, to save the boys.

When all seemed lost, the brothers found a tunnel and escaped. Charlemagne pursued them to Maugis's lands, where they took a hostage – the emperor's best friend. Charlemagne at last agreed to peace, but asked for Bayart in exchange. Tying a stone to the horse's neck, he threw him in the River Meuse. Bayart broke the stone with his shoes, swam to the bank and ran into the forest, mocking his executioner with a happy neigh.

Renaud and Bayart capture their foes.

WILLIAM SHORT-NOSE

Old Aimeri of Narbonne was proud of his six sons. William, the youngest, had won fame by routing some Saracens carrying a message from the Emir of Orange to his betrothed, Princess Oriabel. Learning how beautiful the princess was, William swore to marry her.

Charlemagne, grown old, wished to announce his successor. He summoned his bishops and lords to church and solemnly gave the crown to his son Louis, who was still a child. "Swear to fight my enemies and to help my friends," he said. Louis trembled and refused the golden crown; he hated war. Arnéis, Duke of Orleans, walked forward. He offered to be Louis' tutor for three years. Some cheered as the emperor almost accepted. But Aimeri's sons guessed that Arnéis wanted to

steal the throne. William rushed at the traitor, killed him with a blow of his fist and placed the crown on young Louis' head. Then Charlemagne spoke: "This knight will do great deeds," he proclaimed. "My son, when you are emperor, do not forget him!"

A short time later, the Pope asked William to defend the city of Rome. He killed Giant Corsolt, a Saracen champion, in single combat. But before he died, the giant cut off the tip of William's nose – and gained him the nickname of William Short-Nose.

After the battle, William heard that Charlemagne was dead. A usurper called Acelin had driven Louis to take refuge at Tours. William came to the rescue with 600 men. He defied the rebel army and broke the traitor's skull.

For three years, William fought Saracens and

Saxons. Soon, Louis had no enemies to fear. But William got no lands in reward. Pale with rage, he entered the palace with a clatter of leather boots. In defiance, he broke his bow in Louis' face. Proud William asked for lands the Saracens held: Nîmes, Orange and the kingdom of Spain. Louis gave William his glove to show he agreed.

To win his lands, William recruited young men, who brought whatever armor they could afford. Many were on foot or on shabby horses, but all longed to prove their worth.

William dressed up as a merchant and hid his men in barrels to conquer the city of Nîmes. Then he marched on Orange; he had not forgotten the Emir's beautiful wife. Oriabel was locked up in a tower called Gloriette and hated the old Emir. Disguised again, William visited her. His heart was won by her beauty, and he revealed who he was. She welcomed him and helped the Franks to take Orange. The Emir died in the battle. Oriabel was baptized and

married William. William and Oriabel faced the Saracens side by side. One day, their foolhardy nephew, Vivien, rode against a huge Saracen force. William went to his aid, but was too late: the Saracens had landed at Aliscans. Vivien was mortally wounded. William put on Saracen armor and escaped. Soon after, the Saracens besieged Orange. William slipped out to seek reinforcements, while Oriabel and her women put on armor to defend the town.

Louis was feasting and did not seem to care. William let his anger show again. At last, Louis promised help. Back at Orange, William wept aloud. The town was in ruins; only the tower Gloriette stood, held by his wife. Oriabel tenderly took him in her arms. At last, the king's army came. The Saracens sent a witch against them. Giant Rainouart, Oriabel's brother, drove them off with a sword mounted on a tree trunk. The Saracens returned to their ships in disarray.

The Saracens had landed on the beach!

43

CHIVALRY, TRUE AND FALSE

Chivalry means the code of knighthood, the rules and ideals knights followed and, more generally, knights and their stories themselves. Today it is sometimes used to mean good manners, unselfishness and courage, all of which medieval knights were supposed to practice.

The idea of chivalry is very old. In the Middle Ages, as long ago as the 1100s, people were making up stories about knights of "long ago." They contained romance and excitement, instruction in morals and manners and increasingly, religious symbolism. In those days before printing, such stories were read often aloud in the halls of lords and kings. People did not believe them literally even then, but delighted in the entertainment they provided and the high ideals they represented.

Modern historians believe that the medieval knights originated in the time of Charlemagne (see page 28). Some came from the old Frankish aristocracy, others from a new group of people enriched by royal grants of land given in thanks for service in war. At that time, much of Europe was pagan, and some knightly traditions – in myth as well as reality – stem from the customs of Germanic warriors which go back long before the Holy Roman Empire. One example is the custom whereby a young warrior would pledge his service to an older one, who would then provide him with horse, weapons and keep.

Horses and armor

Our image of the knight today would hardly be complete without his armor, his sword, shield and lance, and above all, his horse. Knights traveled and fought on horseback, and knighthood could hardly have developed without the invention of the stirrup, which gave the knight the ability to move about in the saddle without too much risk of falling off. The knight would grip his lance and ride against his opponent with enormous force – the weight of his horse being added to his own.

The horse had to be a big, strong animal – the size of a modern cart horse, though presumably faster on its feet – to carry the weight of a fully-armed knight during long hard battles. The iron horseshoe, which protects the hooves and helps the horse keep its footing in difficult terrain, is an invention of the early Middle Ages.

The knights of this early period wore solid iron helmets and body armor of chain mail. It was made by hand, a long and complicated process in which wire was coiled around a rod, then cut down one side of the rod to make a great many open rings. The ends of the ring were hammered flat. Then the rings were linked to make "fabric" and the flattened ends riveted together. A suit of chain mail was a valuable possession.

Along with his broad sword, a knight might carry a light lance and an axe, and would wear spurs – a symbol of his status as well as a means of controlling his horse. His shield was made of wood covered with leather, painted with a symbol to allow him to be recognized by his own side. These symbols – at first simple designs of one or two colors and a "metal" background – grew into the complicated art of heraldry, in which "coats of arms" belonged to the heads of particular families, sometimes with a rather contrived joke on the family's name or history, and were "quartered" with other arms to mark marriages. Late medieval coats of arms, with four or even eight designs of many colors on the same shield, would have been useless for the original purpose of quick recognition in war.

A brutal life

All these heavy iron weapons suggest the sad truth about knighthood; it was a very violent way of life. The graceful, romantic and well-mannered Sir Lancelot and Sir Gawain would hardly have survived long in the brutal reality of medieval warfare. Real early knights lived in often-squalid castles, settled disputes about land with the sword, and

were illiterate, rough and greedy.

Some of the Charlemagne stories give an idea of the sheer unpleasantness of siege warfare, in which an army would surround a castle or walled city and try to enter it with ladders and battering-rams or break down the walls or kill the defenders with huge stones fired from catapults. If they did not succeed, they would wait until the inhabitants had starved to death.

Meanwhile, the defenders inside would try to drive the enemy away by such techniques as pouring boiling oil down on their heads. An "impregnable" castle, with high thick walls and no windows except tiny arrow-slots, must have been a mixed blessing; it was very difficult to get out of when overwhelmed by enemies, and conditions inside during a siege must rapidly have become revolting, with no proper sewers and many wounded or dead.

Knighthood and the Church

At the end of the AD 900s, the Church became concerned about the violence of life all over Europe. In AD 987 a council of bishops proclaimed the Peace of God, threatening anyone who plundered a church, struck an unarmed priest or robbed a peasant or poor man, with expulsion from the Church. Knights and nobles were called to assemblies, where they swore oaths on holy relics to keep the peace. Similar councils over the next half-century may not have really improved the knights' behavior, but knighthood became associated with the Church as a result. A council in 1054 proclaimed: "Let no Christian kill another Christian, for there is no doubt that he who kills a Christian spills the blood of Christ."

The suggestion was that war was only justified when carried out against the "enemies of Christ." The way was paved for the Crusades. On November 27, 1095, Pope Urban II preached in an open field in central France, encouraging his flock to ride to Jerusalem and take it away from the Saracens (Moslem

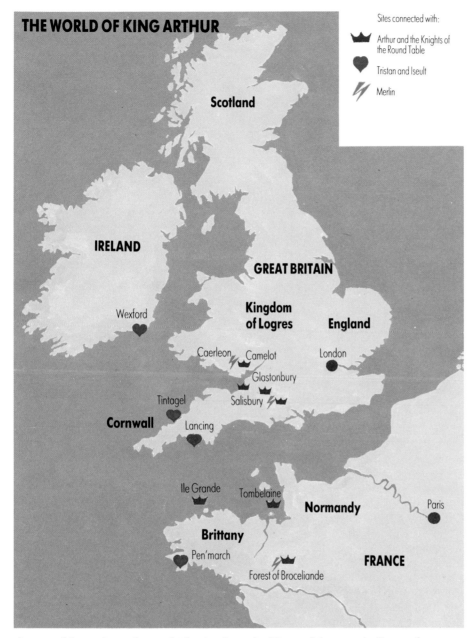

THE WORLD OF KING ARTHUR

Sites connected with:

Arthur and the Knights of the Round Table

Tristan and Iseult

Merlin

Scotland

IRELAND

GREAT BRITAIN

Wexford

Kingdom of Logres

England

Caerleon

Camelot

London

Glastonbury

Tintagel

Salisbury

Cornwall

Lancing

Ile Grande

Tombelaine

Normandy

Paris

Brittany

Pen'march

FRANCE

Forest of Broceliande

A map of the settings of some Arthurian legends. Many of them are in France because the original authors came from there.

The legends of Arthur

Arthur takes us back a long way from the Crusades. It is very difficult to squeeze a little reality from the mass of legends, but he may have been a Celtic chieftain who defended part of Britain from the Germanic ("Saxon") invaders who came in the wake of the withdrawal of Roman troops from Britain in the late AD 500s. He is associated with Wales and the West Country above all, and South Cadbury, an Iron Age fortress in Wiltshire, excavated during the 1970s, which is just possibly the site of the original "Camelot." But there are "Camelots," "Arthur's Seats" and "Arthur's Camps" all over Britain, not just in the western parts. Recently, a site under a former factory in Scotland was suggested as a new contender for the honor of being the "real" Camelot.

The legends said that at the end of his reign, Arthur was carried in a boat to the Isle of Avalon, where he did not die, but remained forever. Many scholars have suggested that Avalon was the land "island" of Glastonbury, in Wiltshire.

By the rules of courtly love, a knight had to earn his lady's favor.

knights) who occupied it.

The eight Crusades which followed were, in truth, no more holy than any other medieval wars; many Crusaders were there for plunder and to settle old scores as much as to reclaim the holy city for the Christians, and the battles were as bloody as secular ones. But the Crusades led to the setting-up of Orders of Knighthood such as the Templars, which emphasized duty and brotherhood (even if less in practice than in theory), and influenced the writers'

picture of Arthur's and Charlemagne's knights.

Ironically, the very Moslems the Crusaders were fighting were perhaps the nearest thing in real life to the legendary knights. Moslem cavalry techniques were gladly adopted by early Christian armies, and the Prophet Mohammed's concept of *jihad*, Holy War, was something they seriously believed in. In some ways, the intensely religious Sir Percival is more like a Saracen than many real-life Christian knights.

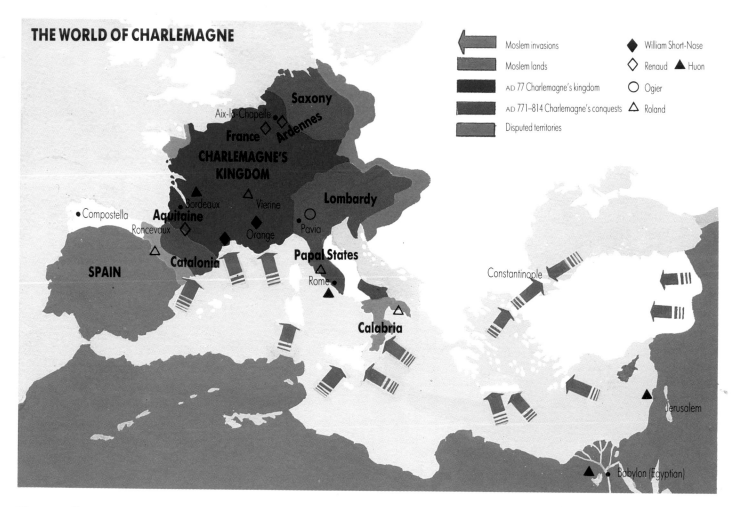

THE WORLD OF CHARLEMAGNE

Saxony
Aix-la-Chapelle
France Ardennes
CHARLEMAGNE'S
KINGDOM
Lombardy
• Compostella Bordeaux Vienne
Aquitaine
Roncevaux Orange Pavia
SPAIN Catalonia Papal States
Rome •
Constantinople
Calabria
Jerusalem
Babylon (Egyptian)

◄ Moslem invasions   ◆ William Short-Nose
  Moslem lands   ◇ Renaud ▲ Huon
  AD 77 Charlemagne's kingdom ○ Ogier
  AD 771–814 Charlemagne's conquests △ Roland
  Disputed territories

From reality to romance

The ultimate origin of the Arthur stories – apart from this now-forgotten chieftain – is found in Celtic stories such as the *Mabinogion*. Early chroniclers were using the name Arthur for the leader of the British forces before AD 800. But strangely enough, the great flowering of Arthurian romance was inspired by a French book dedicated to Henry II's queen, Eleanor of Aquitaine, who was also Queen of France.

Robert Wace, a French priest, finished his book in 1155. It was a verse translation of *The History of the Kings of Britain*, a Latin chronicle by Geoffrey of Monmouth. The Round Table first appears in Wace's French version. Wace inspired writers at the French court to embroider the subject in romances which set out their own ideals of perfect (fictional) knighthood.

Among them was Chrétien de Troyes, who wrote five romances whose heroes are wandering knights. German poets such as Wolfram von Eschenbach wrote Arthurian stories, too, giving added importance to the Holy Grail. In the 1200s, a French author whose name is unknown produced a long prose collection of the stories, now called the Vulgate Cycle. This was an important source for Sir Thomas Malory, who around 1470 wrote *Morte d'Arthur*, astonishingly enough the first written appearance of the story of Arthur in English.

Alongside the courtly, written stories, there were a great many folk tales about Arthur, often associated with particular places where he was said to have done some great deed. There are many different versions of a story in which a poor man blunders into a cave, where he sees the sleeping figures of Arthur and his knights, waiting to be woken when their country needs to be saved from danger. Similar "sleepers' cave" stories are told about the great Charlemagne of France.

The map shows the warring kingdoms at the time of Charlemagne, and the places where his knights fought.

Charlemagne

Charlemagne's grandfather, Charles Martel, became famous for stopping a Moslem invasion at Poitiers in AD 732. His father, Pepin the Short, was elected king in AD 751 and crowned in AD 754. At his death in AD 768, he divided his kingdom between his two sons, Charles and Carloman.

Charles, the elder, was 26 when he became king. He inherited part of Aquitaine along with the rest of his lands. This province was soon in revolt against his rule. He rapidly subdued the rebels, although his brother Carloman refused to help.

On Carloman's death in AD 771, Charles took his territory, dispossessing his nephews, who fled to Lombardy. Charles the Great – Charlemagne – was now King of all France.

During his reign, he fought many wars to secure the frontiers of France. Every spring, he called his vassals (lords who had sworn to serve him) and their armies together, to fight until the beginning of winter.

First, he campaigned against the Lombards, whose king surrendered after the siege of Pavia. Wearing their traditional iron crown, Charlemagne was crowned King of Lombardy in AD 774. Three years later, he fought the Saxons, but it took him nearly 30 years to overcome these pagan peoples. The war was very cruel.

Meanwhile, Charlemagne crossed the Pyrénées to fight the Saracens. This expedition led to the disaster at Roncevaux in AD 778, which became celebrated many years later in the *Song of Roland*. Fifteen years later the Emir Escham declared a Holy War, and his Saracens invaded the south of France. The Franks, commanded by William of Aquitaine, drove them away and then marched down into Spain, where they seized Barcelona in AD 801.

Religion and learning

On Christmas Day AD 800, the Pope proclaimed Charlemagne Emperor of the West. Henceforth, Charlemagne regarded himself as the defender of the Church. He encouraged the foundation of monasteries and abbeys and obliged every monastery to open a school. He also encouraged the spread of classical and early Christian books.

The emperor loved learning and knew some Latin and Greek, but he never learned to write.

The *Chansons de Geste*

Charlemagne died in AD 814, and a scholar who was a friend of his wrote a biography of him. The emperor had been an impressive and memorable ruler. In the following centuries, poets embroidered the history of his time and invented characters who sometimes became more famous than the real people.

For example, Bertrade, the emperor's real mother, became "Berthe," daughter of an imaginary king of Hungary. Roland, presented as Charlemagne's nephew, was in fact no relation. In these epic poems, the emperor has twelve nobles, knights of high lineage who perform great deeds. One was Ogier the Dane, probably inspired by a duke who defended Charlemagne's nephews when they fled to Lombardy; another was Oliver, an imaginary hero, but as famous as his friend Roland. The Saracens are represented on an epic scale, the biggest giants and the wickedest criminals ever seen.

These legends inspired the *Chansons de Geste*, written at the time of the Crusades, two or three centuries after the emperor's death. It was then the fashion to exalt the courage of Christian knights fighting the Moslems.

Victorian chivalry

The real knights died out in the 1400s, with the introduction of gunpowder and other changes. Romances about them were popular for many years, and kings such as Henry VIII still rode in spectacular tournaments, though these were sporting rather than real military occasions. Gradually, the very idea of knighthood began to seem woefully old-fashioned. That great classic of Spanish literature, *Don Quixote* (1604), shows the noble but ridiculous old knight fighting windmills under the impression that they are giants.

In the late 1700s, scholars began to be interested in the Middle Ages, learning the languages of the time and trying to save books and other objects of interest. Chivalry, too, became a popular subject, especially in the following century. The novels of Sir Walter Scott (1771-1832) about medieval life became immensely popular.

In the reign of Queen Victoria of England, chivalry became the rage, with upper-class young people even dressing up as knights and holding "tournaments" for fun. Alfred, Lord Tennyson – the Poet Laureate and the best-selling poet of the time, wrote many Arthurian poems, including *The Lady of Shallot* and *Idylls of the King*. Later, the socialist poet and designer, William Morris, who used medieval styles as the inspiration for his own, wrote *The Defense of Guinevere*. In this poem, the queen, accused of unfaithfulness, stands up bravely to her prosecutors. She comes across as a strong and real person, not a mere "damsel in

The story of Renaud killing Charlemagne's nephew with a chess-board has no basis in history. It is the subject of one of the Chansons de Geste.

distress."

During World War I, the young men who died in the trenches were portrayed on postcards and magazine illustrations as knights in shining armor, fighting for right until death. The reality of trench warfare was as different from this charming image as medieval warfare had been.

A modern Camelot

Arthur's legend has kept its power even to modern times. When John Fitzgerald Kennedy was elected president in 1960, people began to compare this young intelligent leader with a beautiful wife with Arthur and referred to his "court" as Camelot. When Kennedy was shot by an assassin in 1963, the world mourned his death and looked on his time as a lost golden age, just as Medieval Britain longed for the Age of Arthur.

INDEX